Amazing Faith

Above and Beyond Extraordinary

Pastor Michael Tyree

Copyright © 2023 by Michael Tyree

All rights reserved. No portion of this book may be reproduced in any form without written permission from the publisher or author, except as permitted by U.S. copyright law.

This publication is designed to provide accurate and authoritative information in regard to the subject matter covered. It is sold with the understanding that neither the author nor the publisher is engaged in rendering legal, investment, accounting or other professional services. While the publisher and author have used their best efforts in preparing this book, they make no representations or warranties with respect to the accuracy or completeness of the contents of this book and specifically disclaim any implied warranties of merchantability or fitness for a particular purpose. No warranty may be created or extended by sales representatives or written sales materials. The advice and strategies contained herein may not be suitable for your situation. You should consult with a professional when appropriate. Neither the publisher nor the author shall be liable for any loss of profit or any other commercial damages, including but not limited to special, incidental, consequential, personal, or other damages. Any questions or for bulk ordering, email: pastortyreeofficial@gmail.com

Unless noted otherwise, scripture quotation is from New International King James Version of the Holy Bible.

Printed in the United States of America

ISBN: 9798337947389

Photographer: Brandi Myers

Library of Congress Data in Progress

Cover Design – MTGRAPHIX CREATIVE GROUP

Table of Contents

Dedication	VII
Preface	VIII
Foreword	X
1. Introduction	1
2. Beginner's Faith	3
3. Grandma's Prayers	10
4. Miracle Money	16
5. Seeds of Blessings	22
6. Finding Faith in Unexpected Places	28
7. Faithful in the Process	34
8. Faith Works	39
9. When God Shows Up and Shows Out	45
10. Leap of Faith	51
11. An Unexpected Blessing	57
12. It's Time for a Miracle	64
13. Faith for the Family	70
About the Author	76

"NOW FAITH IS THE SUBSTANCE OF THINGS HOPED FOR, THE EVIDENCE OF THINGS NOT SEEN."

HEBREWS 11:1 (KJV)

Dedication

To MY WIFE AND bride of 36 years, my ebony queen, the lovely Lady Dyan Tyree.

To my amazingly talented children, my daughter, Deanna Marie Tyree, aka "DeeMarie" and my son, Michael Eric James Tyree aka "Mike Teezy", to my beautiful granddaughter, little Ms. Nevaeh Tyree.

A special dedication to my grandfather, the late Rev. Eric "Step" Tyree, and my uncle, the late Rev. Eric Donald Tyree.

To the entire Tyree Tribe, to my late Grandma Ms. Amanda "Tootsie" Tyree - "I miss you so much!" To my mother, the Rev. Marykaye Jacquet, Aunt Rosetta Conroy, cousin Dawn Conroy, additional family Auntie "BB" – Mrs. Beverly Robinson and Aunt Teresa Tyree - Schofied.

To my siblings, Joseph Cook and family, Marianne Spottswood and family, Jonathan Carruth and Daughter.

And to all my extended Johnson family.

I also dedicate this book to those of you who are reading it and choosing to activate your faith.

Preface

TODAY I WAS GIVEN the privilege and opportunity to review a few chapters of what I believe is one of the most inspirational, motivational books on having not just Faith in God (trusting and believing God) but having the Faith of God.

This book is readable, relatable, rational, and revelatory. While reading it, there is no way one would believe that it was written by a first-time author but rather by a seasoned scripter with astute journalistic abilities who can take you off the pages of the stories and place you into the moment: the day, hour, and setting that these Amazing Faith experiences have taken place.

What gives the book such an edge is that it is a combination of true-to-life stories, events, and people who trusted in the God of might and miracles and dared to believe He would work a faith miracle in their lives. This book spans generations that can ignite a little boy's faith whose desire to play guitar activated that desire to trust God for the money to purchase that guitar. It speaks to millennials and young adult couples who are gifted, have good morals, and are willing to work a job but have difficulty believing they can be hired and paid for what they are worth. And then it speaks to people of all ages who perhaps may have trusted God in one season of their lives but over time and circumstances have stopped believing as strongly as they use to; maybe they are in that "God I want to believe but help my unbelief stage." These chapters will, no doubt, reawaken and reacquaint the reader with the faith in the God who can not only change the denominations of copper metal coins but can change their metallic configuration into a fabric that first started as wood fibers or plastics into the currency we use in exchange for those things that we can buy...while giving God the Glory for purchasing salvation for us with the currency of heaven.

I cannot wait for the book release to get my hands on the entire publication. I am overwhelmed with pride, tears, and exhilaration for the author, and for his skillful ability to put such a masterful work into the hands of those who I know will share my sentiments when reading the first few chapters.

What I am most excited about and Godly proud of is that the author is also my beloved son, with whom I am well pleased.

God, thank you for your guiding hand, fierce love, and inspiration that you have poured out in abundance on my son's life. There is no greater delight for a mother, than to know that her son is Your son, modeling the Faith given by his Father, God in Heaven.

Minister Marykaye Jacquet

Foreword

I AM HONORED AND privileged to write the foreword for Pastor Michael Tyree's debut book, *Amazing Faith Above and Beyond Extraordinary*. I have had the pleasure of knowing Pastor Tyree for almost three decades, and during this time, I have seen the profound impact his faith in God has had on his life, his family, his church, and the lives of those around him.

In this book, Pastor Tyree shares his journey of faith, from the valleys to the mountaintops, and the incredible experiences he has encountered along the way. His testimonies will challenge you to step out of your comfort zone and trust God in every circumstance.

Pastor Tyree's unwavering faith in God has inspired me to believe in God for the impossible. I have seen the transformative power of his faith in action, and I am confident that as you read these pages, you will be encouraged to trust God and attempt great things.

I hope that *Amazing Faith Above and Beyond Extraordinary* will inspire you to embrace a more excellent life of faith and to trust in God's promises. May you be inspired, empowered, and blessed by this incredible book.

Bishop Shawn Branham

Senior Pastor, Trailblazers Church

Introduction

First, I want to thank you for making the conscious decision to read this book. Trust me, this is not a coincidence. You're about to embark upon an amazing journey of faith and discover a new level of trust in God as I share some outstanding testimonies.

My personal journey with faith all began at 307 Morris Avenue where my grandfather built a house with his own hands. We lived in the small town of Beckley, West Virginia. This little house was popular in our neighborhood. It became known as "Holy Ghost Headquarters," because the word got out that God was moving and meeting us there.

In this small house, miracles were taking place, people were getting filled with the Spirit, and there was always a mighty move of God.

People were frequently gathering around the kitchen table, singing songs of praise, or giving testimony and talking about the goodness of the Lord. Even though there was a lot of focus on God, our family still knew how to have fun.

I will never forget how my grandfather taught me to play the card game UNO. He'd routinely make a cough-like sound, as he laid down his card. He would cough and then say, "Getcha-Two!"

Nowadays, it seems that many people are so consumed with electronics such as cell phones and computers that they forget about the joy of just spending time with their families.

People were often coming from and going to our house. My grandparents knew no strangers. Everyone was always welcome! If you came to visit, then you might as well prepare to stay for a while, and enjoy a good meal, some good conversation, and prepare for a spontaneous worship experience! My family taught me the principles of faith and the value of prayer.

My grandparents were loving, kindhearted, and very influential in my life. They stepped up and stepped in to help my mother raise my brother, Joseph, and me. They served as pillars in the community and dedicated their lives to the calling of ministry. My grandfather was a Baptist pastor, and my grandmother served as the First Lady of the church.

This was the beginning of my foundation of faith. They laid the bricks for the wall of prayer, which became the foundation of my faith, and trusting God which enabled me to have the testimonies that you're about to read in the next few pages of this book.

I had my first encounter with God in this house, in West Virginia, at the age of nine. This experience literally changed my life forever. As you read my amazing testimonies of faith, I hope it not only changes your life but transforms your faith so that you can learn to walk in *Amazing Faith – Above and Beyond Extraordinary*.

Beginner's Faith

*Be faithful in small things because
it is in them that your strength lies.*

Mother Teresa

I grew up in the church. I was always around good music, folks who sang, and those who played music exceptionally well. I never will forget musician Anton Snyder who would come over to our house and wear the piano out.

My aunts, Beverly and Teresa, were also both extraordinary psalmists and piano players. They had many friends who were musically inclined and stopped by often to share their gifts and talents with the family. By being exposed to music at such an early age, I fell in love with the guitar. We had a phenomenal guitarist, by the name of Kenny Morris, at the church I attended. When I listened to him play, I would get lost in the music. He inspired me to want to learn to play the guitar.

One day, my grandparents took me window shopping at Raines Music Store in Beckley, West Virginia. They didn't have the money to buy a guitar at that time and I was too young to get a job and earn the money to buy one.

Even though we were just supposed to be window shopping, I had this thing called "Amazing Faith." I had been listening to my grandfather's sermons on the topic of faith and had learned the power of believing and standing on God's Word.

By this time, I was ready to put my grandfather's sermons into action.

I remembered my grandfather preaching about the woman with the issue of blood. Mark Chapter 5 gives a woman's testimony of dealing with the issue of blood. She had been struggling for 12 years but she had enough faith to believe that if she could just touch the hem of Jesus' garment, she would be completely healed and made whole. The scripture that stood out in my mind was *"And he said unto her, Daughter, thy faith hath made thee whole; go in peace, and be whole of thy plague."* **(Mark 5:34)**

What I took away from that sermon was priceless. I learned that anything is possible if I laid hold of it in the Spirit. All things are possible to them that believe.

My faith had been activated to believe!

While we were shopping, I spotted the guitar I wanted. It was $160.00. I touched it, and by actually laying my hands on it, l claimed it in the Spirit. I knew it was mine; I just didn't know how or when. I had no idea how soon my faith could bring this to fruition.

My grandmother was a little frightened about my eagerness and said that the store manager might think I was trying to steal the guitar. She said, "Boy, get your hands off that guitar – these folks don't know nothing about laying hands and claiming things!"

After leaving the store, I prayed and asked the Lord to give me direction on how to get the money together to buy this guitar.

Later that day, the Lord directed me to visit my cousin Eugene and see if there were any household chores I could assist him with to earn money. My grandparents also taught me the value of a good work ethic and that if you want anything in life, you have to be willing to work hard for it.

Cousin Eugene was an elderly gentleman who was very quiet, stayed to himself often, and he liked to drink a little bit. We're not talking Kool-Aid if you know what I mean.

I knocked on the door and said, "Cousin Eugene, do you have any chores that I can help you with to raise money? I want to buy a guitar so that I can play for the Lord!"

Cousin Eugene pondered for a few moments. Then he said, "Can you run a vacuum cleaner and sweep my floors?"

"Yes, sir!" I exclaimed.

After cleaning all the floors, he gave me $50.00!

Filled with so much excitement, I did not waste another minute. I struck while the iron was hot. "Cousin Eugene, is there anything else I can do?" I eagerly said.

He asked me to empty the trash cans, and I did it. BAM! He gave me another $50.00!

Oh boy, my faith was on fire!

I had to try it again! "Cousin Eugene, is there anything else I can do for you?" I asked.

He said, "What about shining my shoes?"

He was a sharp dresser, so he had about twenty pairs of shoes. I shined them all – every last pair. POW! Another $50.00!

As a young man, this was an eye-opening experience about faith. As you can imagine, all this happened on the same day! I am completely amazed at how quickly the Lord responded to my faith and answered my prayer.

After making $150.00, I was full of excitement. I ran all the way home. My faith was on fire and so was I. I didn't even knock and busted the door down screaming, "I got it, I got it! Grandma, I got it, I got it!"

She said, "Slow down, got what, son?"

Without taking a breath, I said, "I've got the money to go get my guitar."

She said, "Wait one minute...where did you get that kind of money?"

I said, "Cousin Eugene!"

She said, "Oh Lord, boy, do you know that he's got a drinking problem and may not be aware of what he's doing?"

My grandmother called cousin Eugene to verify that he had actually given me the money. He said, "Tootsie, I gave the boy the money to buy that guitar, so he can play it for the Lord."

The rest is history. And that's how I got my first guitar. I learned to activate my faith.

To God be the Glory!

Points of Faith

- **All things are possible to them that believe.**

Jesus said unto him, "If thou canst believe, all things are possible to him that believeth."

(Mark 9:23)

- **God responds quickly to faith! If you can believe it, then you can achieve it!**

And all things whatsoever ye shall ask in prayer, believing, ye shall receive."

(Matthew 21:22)

- **Faith causes you to lay hold on it in the Spirit – before you obtain it physically.**

As it is written: *"I have made thee a father of many nations"), in the presence of Him whom he believed, even God, who quickeneth the dead and calleth those things which are not, as though they were."* **(Romans 4:17**

Prayer

Lord, I understand that faith is a process. I ask you for the strength to step out of who I am and walk into whom you want me to be. It is my desire to trust you not just for big things but for every little thing in my life. Lord, let me open my heart to experience faith in a new way. Every day allow me to strengthen my faith muscles as I grow closer to you.

Grandma's Prayers

*Your grandmother's prayers are still
protecting you.*

Lana Delia

My grandmother was the pillar of our family. She was an outstanding homemaker and an anointed woman of prayer and power. Not many people knew it, but Grandmother carried a strong prophetic anointing on her life.

My grandparents were Baptist people who just loved God and fell in love with serving the needs of others. They were always opening their doors to family, friends, neighbors, and even strangers. They were constantly sharing the light of God's love with everyone they met.

One day, my grandparents had an encounter with God and were filled with the Holy Spirit. The news began to spread like wildfire. People started coming from everywhere to this little house, 307 Morris Avenue, to receive, touch, and encounter the Spirit. After that point, the house was known as Holy Ghost Headquarters.

Fast forward, I am married to my beautiful wife Dyan, and we have two children that bring us so much joy. But we are not exempt from trouble and struggle.

There was a time in my life that we were going through a transition. Desperately in need of a job, I applied at several places, and nothing seemed to be opening up or coming through for me. I had been trying all day to find employment and was getting discouraged.

I went to apply at One Valley Bank in Charleston, West Virginia. I was interviewed by a nice professional woman, Ms. Kidd, only to hear her say, "Mr. Tyree, I'm sorry...we have nothing available; your credit score is too low to work here."

I was frustrated and discouraged as I went home feeling defeated. I decided to visit my grandmother on the way home. I shared with her that I had fallen on tough times, and they seemed to be getting tougher.

"Grandma, nobody wants to hire me. You have to have good credit in order to get a good job," I said with discouragement.

Immediately, it was as if Grandma got a download in the Spirit! She said, "Oh no, son, I hear the Lord saying go back, go back, and try it again!"

Frustrated and confused, I said, "But Grandma..."

My grandmother wasn't hearing my "buts." She was adamant in her faith and said, "Go back!"

Not only was my grandmother's faith tenacious, but it was also contagious.

I began to change my attitude by saying to myself, "Lord, I thank you for my new job!" Every step I took on my way back to the bank, I just kept repeating, "Lord, I thank you for my new job!"

Finally, I arrived back at the bank. I explained to Ms. Kidd how desperate I was and I needed a job to take care of my family. I also said something like, "How can I fix my credit if no one is willing to hire me?"

Ms. Kidd said, "I'm sorry there's nothing I can do."

But this time around, I learned to maintain my faith. I kept saying to myself, "Lord, I thank you for my new job."

On my way out the door, I said to myself, "Lord, I thank you for my new job." I kept repeating it over and over. Within seconds of walking away from her, Mrs. Kidd called me back inside.

She ran down the hall and said, "Mr. Tyree, come back. I just remembered someone has resigned from the mailroom and you don't need good credit to work there."

Well, what do you know, my grandmother's faith was spot-on. She hit the nail on the head. I started out in the mailroom and worked my way all the way up to the Human Resources Department, where folks are hired and fired. God gave me favor, and I worked at that company for approximately 22 years.

Points of Faith

- **Faith is contagious! It spreads like wildfire.**

"Go ye therefore and teach all nations, baptizing them in the name of the Father, and of the Son, and of the Holy Ghost, teaching them to observe all things whatsoever I have commanded you. And lo, I am with you always, even unto the end of the world." Amen. (Mathew 28; 19-20)

- **Don't be afraid to trust God again! Maybe it just wasn't the right time before. Go back and try it again.**

"Immediately the boy's father exclaimed, "I do believe; help me overcome my unbelief!" (Mark 9:24)

- **A changed mind changes everything, especially the end result.**

"Fear not, for I am with you; be not dismayed, for I am your God; I will strengthen you, I will help you, I will uphold you with my righteous right hand. (Isaiah 41:10)

Prayer

Lord, sometimes it is not always easy to have faith in the things that I know you have in store for me. Please allow me to surround myself with people who will speak faith into my spirit. Let me boldly speak to those things that are not and call them into existence as though they already are established, In Jesus' name.

Miracle Money

*Life is a series of thousands of
tiny miracles.*

Mike Greenberg

I'm not really sure who is responsible for getting the credit, for creating the phrase "Miracle Money." No matter who coined the phrase, I am going to have to borrow it for this chapter.

Buckle your seat belts, and get ready, for what I am about to share with you is nothing less than the absolute truth.

One morning, around 5:30 a.m., the Spirit of the Lord woke me up and told me to get up and start cleaning the house. I clearly remember Him telling me that He wanted to show me something.

All I could think was this was awesome. The first thing that I wanted to do was to share this moment with my wife. I woke her up and told her the Lord said to clean the house. With her eyes slanted in a hint of attitude and anger from the early disturbance, she said, "He didn't tell me, He told you." She turned over and went back to sleep.

I was determined not to miss God. And even though it was really early, I still got up. I was looking forward to this one-on-one time with God. I had no idea what He was about to share with me nor the extraordinary miracle that was about to take place right before my eyes.

As I was cleaning the house, I noticed a few pennies lodged in the dirt that I had swept up. I heard a voice that said, "You don't need no dirty pennies." This was obviously, the adversary.

You may remember seeing a cartoon, where there's a little red devil on one shoulder and a little white angel on the other shoulder. They are both battling it out to see who is going to get control of the person.

This moment that I'm sharing with you is similar to that scenario. Immediately, after hearing the enemy's voice, I heard another voice say, "Pick 'em up" (referring to the dirty pennies). Then as I picked up the pennies, I heard the Spirit say to make a declaration over the pennies. As I picked up the pennies, I made the declaration, "I will never be broke another day in my life." I didn't just say it to myself, I said it out loud. I said it loud enough that my words echoed off the walls of the house.

After cleaning the entire house, I had a total of seven dirty pennies. In hindsight, I learned that money doesn't lose its value just because it may be looked down upon as being dirty, the scum of the earth, or in a low place. And people don't either. Don't let the low place fool you. When God has a purpose and a plan for your life, no matter how low you go, God has a way of lifting you up out of the gutter and placing you in your rightful place.

Well, the number seven means the completion of God's perfection. I took those dirty seven pennies and placed them in my wallet. Before that, my wallet was empty.

As the cleaning continued, it was almost time for me to go to work. Well, I was broke; the seven pennies were all I had. I needed gas money. So, I called my close friend David to borrow five dollars to get money for gas.

Here's where the miracle took place.

David came to the house and gave me five dollars. As I opened up my wallet, to place the money that David had just given me inside, I noticed a crisp five-dollar bill with two pennies. God had just performed a miracle and given me "Miracle Money." I

couldn't believe it! God had just blown my mind! He took five pennies and miraculously turned them into a brand new five- dollar bill. What a mighty God we serve.

Whenever I share this testimony, people either believe it or they don't. Of course, it's not the monetary value of this testimony that makes it so amazing. It's in the miracle itself that God took something that was worth so little and gave it a greater value.

This lesson is about more than money. God does the same transformation with people. Sin has a way of depreciating our value. However, while we were still in a sinful state, God saw our potential, restored His purpose, and increased our worth.

Another important thing I've learned is to pick up those discarded coins. How many times have you gone to the gas station and found dirty coins scattered all over the place? Pick 'em up and make your own declaration. You don't know, you just may have stumbled upon your next miracle!

God still performs miracles!

Points of Faith

- **Take the limits off God and take the limits off your faith!**

"He replied, "Because you have so little faith. Truly I tell you, if you have faith as small as a mustard seed, you can say to this mountain, 'Move from here to there,' and it will move. Nothing will be impossible for you." (Matthews 17:20)

- **Don't be afraid to let me, the Spirit, guide you!**

"When the Spirit of truth comes, he will guide you into all the truth, for he will not speak on his own authority, but whatever he hears he will speak, and he will declare to you the things that are to come." (John 16:13)

- **Again, take the limits off God and take the limits off your faith!**

I can do all things through him who strengthens me. (Philippians 4:13)

Prayer

Good morning, Holy Spirit! Let's start each and every day together. Let me open the very essence of my soul to not just hear you but trust and obey. Keep me from being afraid to step out into the deep waters to follow your voice. Allow me to from faith to faith as I pursue you with crazy faith.

Seeds of Blessings

*Faith and prayer are the vitamins
of the soul; man cannot live in
health without them.*

Mahalia Jackson

As I begin to review my journey, I've noticed a distinct pattern. It seems as though the enemy has always fought against my prophetic promise, that one day I would be one of God's billionaires.

I want to share with you one of those moments. My wife and I were young in our marriage with two small children. At the time, they were probably two and three years, and still in Pampers.

I had just been laid off from my job. I had received my final paycheck from my employer. This was on a Friday and we had a church service to attend that night.

Dyan and I decided that we would attend the service and take our kids with us. The service was uplifting and we were enjoying ourselves. Then it was offertory time. The Lord spoke to me as people were walking around to collect money in the offering tray. He said, "Give me your check."

I thought to myself, *Oh boy...Lord, are you sure?* Then I said, *Lord, I need you to talk to your daughter sitting next to me* (referring to my wife).

I shared what I heard. Immediately, my wife goes off, "Boy you done lost your mind. Ain't no way God told you that...these babies need Pampers and milk."

After a moment of sheer panic, she said, "But if God told you, then you better do what He said."

I took a deep breath, endorsed my check to the church, and gave it as unto the Lord!

Little did I know, but there was a true Prophet of God in the house, named Prophet Jimmy Reese in the church. Immediately, after giving the check, he came to me and said, "The Lord said, because of your obedience and willingness to trust Him, I'm sending you money in the mail."

At that precise moment, I'm trying to figure God out and wondering how this is going to happen. The Prophet spoke in that same moment as if he could hear my thoughts. He said, "Stop trying to figure it out and just receive it."

I lifted my hands in total praise and complete surrender as unto the Lord. "I receive it, in Jesus' name," I said.

This was on a Friday night. The following Monday morning, I went to the mailbox and there was cash in an envelope addressed to me. I was in complete awe. At the time, I hadn't acknowledged my calling as a minister. But the letter inside the envelope said, "The Lord told me to send my tithe to you." Once again, I was experiencing "Miracle Money!"

Guess what happened the next day? And the next day? And the next? I received cash in the mail every day for several weeks. God was speaking to folks I didn't know. He met me at the point of my need and performed a miracle out of that one act of obedience unto Him.

Wait, it didn't stop there! Do you remember the story in the Bible where the brook dries up on Elijah? Well, the day came for me. I was all excited and expecting to find money in the mail again, as in days past. I went to the mailbox and it seemed that my brook had dried up! There was no money in the mailbox.

The lesson I learned here is to never fall in love with the way God performs miracles in your life. Take the limits off God and trust Him no matter what.

Just like the brook dries up on Elijah, God allowed it to happen in order to redirect him to the widow in Zarephath, who also was in need of a miracle.

God allowed my mailbox to dry up in order to prove that He can make ways in spite of doors that may close or blessings that have run their course. God has 99,000 other ways to bless you.

This particular day, Mr. O'Connor, my next-door neighbor who doesn't believe in God, said to me, "I hear you've fallen on hard times and I want to be a blessing to you!" He gave me a fifty-dollar bill. My wife and I rejoiced on our way to Big Bear, which was a grocery store on Patrick Street in Charleston, West Virginia.

It gets even better, while shopping in the store. The Spirit tells me to look down and underneath my right foot, there's another brand new, crisp fifty-dollar bill. Can someone shout it out and decree, "Miracle Money!" Your miracle is on the way, Hallelujah!

There's nothing impossible for my God. To God be the Glory!

Points of Faith

- **Obedience is better than sacrifice. Obedience paves the pathway to your next miracle.**

"Now therefore, if ye will obey My voice indeed and keep My covenant, then ye shall be a peculiar treasure unto Me above all people; for all the earth is Mine." (Exodus 19:5)

- **God is faithful! Whatever He's promised, He's well able to perform.**

But the Lord is faithful, and he will strengthen you and protect you from the evil one." (2 Thessalonians 3:3)

- **Stop trying to figure everything out! Just Trust God and watch Him work!**

"Commit thy way unto the Lord; also trust in Him, and He shall bring it to pass." (Psalms 37:5)

Prayer

Lord, I am open to however you want to bless me. Let me always be open to following your direction, even when it might not seem comfortable at the time. Please don't let me be so comfortable with the way you are doing something that I cannot shift to the next direction on how you will move.

Finding Faith in Unexpected Places

If fear is cultivated, it will become stronger; if faith is cultivated, it will achieve mastery.

John Paul Jones

I can remember this like it was yesterday. One morning, I was on my way to get breakfast at McDonald's. This man, who was probably in his early 60s, stopped me. And out of the clear blue, he asked me, "Sir, what church do you go to?"

At first, I was startled by his question. I thought to myself, what would make this man ask me such a question? I was dressed in my everyday attire. I didn't think that there was anything about me that gave an inclination or vibe that I was a pastor.

I have to admit, I was in awe that he would select me out of all the people that were in the fast-food restaurant to come up to and inquire about a church.

I wasn't quite sure of his motive, and I wanted to be discrete. I reached into my pocket and pulled out my business card. Then I carefully placed it in his hand.

He took one look at my business card and noticed my picture on it. Then he said, "Oh wow, you're the pastor."

With a smile on my face, I said, "Yes, I am."

Then he said, "I think I want to come to church with you." I said, "You are welcome, anytime."

When people find out that I'm a pastor, I get this sort of response. They often make promises to come to visit my

church, like it is an obligation. Then I never see them again. Therefore, I really didn't expect to see this guy again.

To my surprise, the next Sunday, he showed up for church. He kept coming. He was there the next Sunday and the next Sunday after that.

I still didn't know much about this man. I just knew him as the man that bumped into me at McDonald's. I later found out that his name was Henry Palmer. By this time, he seemed to be a pretty faithful church attendee.

One Sunday, the service was very high. The presence of the Lord was powerful in the room. Everyone there could feel the Holy Spirit. All of a sudden, my wife got a prophetic unction from the Lord. She walked over to Henry and said, "Sir, I don't know you. But I hear the Lord saying he has a job for you."

We found out months later that this man was homeless and that he had been borrowing cars and bumming rides to church all this time. That's how urgent his need was to hear the Word from the Lord.

The day that he received this message, he told us how he grabbed a hold of this prophetic word from my wife by faith! The Bible says, "Faith comes by hearing and hearing by the word of God." (Romans 10:17) Upon receiving this word, he got up the very next morning at 5:00 a.m. and went to Labor Ready, a temporary agency in the area. He said that he was given an assignment that same day.

Every day, he went to work on time and was faithful to that temporary assignment. Before long, the temporary assignment turned into a permanent position. God gave him favor on this job and he eventually became the supervisor.

After his promotion, he came to church and asked if he could share his testimony. He told the church about his struggle with

homelessness and how he dealt with drug addiction for years. All of this made him unapproachable because of the stench from not bathing.

You could have heard a pin drop in the church, when he said, "Look at me now. There was a time that I wasn't employable. My social security number was so toxic, they would take one look at me and throw my stuff in the trash. Look at me now. The woman of God gave me a word that God had a job for me.

I activated my faith, and I believed it. I got up and went after it."

Henry confessed that before he got his job, he always wanted to pay his tithes but all he had was a little change in his pocket. He put that change in the offering plate. We accepted it and prayed over it.

With tears in his eyes, Henry waved an envelope in the air that he had in his hands. He said, "I am so full right now...because, y'all don't understand...this is the first time in my life that I've received a check, with a "comma" on it!"

By this time, there wasn't a dry eye in the church. We all went up in celebration, praising the Lord for Henry's blessing.

Part two of his testimony is that he had been separated from his wife for about ten years. He began sharing the sermon and messages with his wife, throughout the week over the phone. His desire was to be reconciled with his wife. We prayed over his request. We asked God to restore his relationship with his wife. Several years later, his wife packed up her bags and moved to North Carolina to be with Henry.

To God be the Glory for all the great things He has done.

Points of Faith

- **God can show up anywhere, even at McDonald's.**

"The eyes of the Lord are in every place, beholding the evil and the good." (Proverbs 15:3)

- **You don't have to look like what you have been through.**

"He answered and said, "Lo, I see four men loose, walking in the midst of the fire, and they have no hurt; and the form of the fourth is like the Son of God." (Daniel 3:25)

- **God can do anything but fail.**

"Now unto him that is able to do exceeding abundantly above all that we ask or think, according to the power that worketh in us,

(Ephesians 3:20)

Prayer

I surrender to you, Lord. I surrender who I was, my thoughts and the things that I have done. I know that in you, I am a brand new creature. My faith is new, my hope is new, and my love is new. I put aside all old things that tend to hold me back, as I open myself up to new possibilities of blessing that you are bringing my way. I know that no good thing will be withheld from me.

Faithful in the Process

Faith sees the invisible, believes the unbelievable, and receives the impossible.

Corrie Ten Boom

During my tenure at Branch Banking and Trust (BBT), I met a young man who was probably in his late 50s. I will refer to him as Mr. Fred C. He was one of our top executives within the company. Little did we both know that something would happen, and life would take a turn for the worst for him.

His life is a reminder to me of how you can go from the top to the bottom with a simple chain of events. Within a short period of time, he lost his job, had trouble in his marriage, and his wife ended up leaving. Then he became homeless.

Later, I found out that he had been looking for me and searching for the church where I pastored. He said he was just driving around one day, and the Lord said, "Turn here." So that's how he found my church.

He never really took the time to tell me the details of his situation. I just knew that he needed a place to recover and be restored. Our church believed in the power of faith, being mixed with prayer. One core scripture for our church was Matthews 13:58, "And He did not many mighty works there, because of their unbelief." It has always been my wholehearted belief that faith is God giving you the key to unlocking the doors to the miraculous.

All things are possible to them that believe. "And Jesus, looking upon them, said, With men, it is impossible, but not with God; for with God all things are possible." (Mark 10:27)

Every Sunday, Fred came faithfully to church. He would give the little money that he had to give. He contributed where he could, all the time believing God could make it greater. How many of you know, it's not in the amount that you give? It's about the heart from which it is given. Little becomes much when placed in the hands of an Almighty God. Every week, we would pray with him to build and encourage his faith.

Several months went by. Fred started getting a little weary and devastation began to settle in his spirit.

One night, during Wednesday Bible study, I was ministering on the subject of faith. I spoke about holding on to God's unchanging hand and believing God to move on your behalf. Fred came to me after the service and explained how timely and encouraging this message was for him.

The very next day, he received a call from an employer in Florida, who wanted to hire him. He said to the new employer, "Can I ask you a question.?" Jokingly, he asked, "What took you, guys, so long?"

They responded, "We wanted to hire you for a long time. We just wanted to make you an offer that you couldn't refuse."

Fred got the job. He relocated to Florida but didn't forget his home church. He continued to send his tithes to the ministry until the day of his death. God allowed him to walk in total victory before he died. Even in his transition, God honored his faithfulness.

I will forever be grateful for Fred allowing his loving light to shine for all to see it. He was a faithful and tremendous friend.

Rest in Heaven (RIH), Fred.

To God be the Glory!

Points of Faith

- **Faith is an action word. If you have faith? Hold on to it and keep moving forward while waiting on the Word of God to manifest.**

"For as the body without the spirit is dead, so faith without works is dead also." (James 2:26)

- **God is always working things out behind the scenes.**

"The Lord makes firm the steps of the one who delights in him; though he may stumble, he will not fall, for the Lord upholds him with his hand." (Psalms 37:23-24)

- **We don't know how God is going to do something, we have to trust the process.**

"Trust in the Lord with all thine heart, and lean not unto thine own understanding." (Proverbs 3:5)

Prayer

Even though my life may take many twists and turns, Lord, I am open to whatever plans you have for me. I ask you to erase previously conceived ideas and thoughts from my mind. Please allow me to stay open to however you chose to bless me. I am grateful for the angels you have sent to straighten the pathways of my life. With every step that I take, I breathe in your love and let go of my past.

Faith Works

But without faith it is impossible to please Him. For he that cometh to God must believe that He is, and that He is a rewarder of those who diligently seek Him.

Hebrews 11:6

Usually, when the phone rings before 5:00 a.m., it is not good news. One Saturday morning, we got a call around 3:00 a.m. As I picked up the phone, I tried to prepare my heart for whatever news I might receive. It was then that I got the news that Jimmy Beasley (JB), my wife's younger brother, had been shot sixteen times. He was in critical condition.

Immediately, I gathered my family together. We got on the road and headed to Charleston, West Virginia.

Dyan was very anxious to get to her little brother. As hard as I tried to be calm, the temptation to panic was in the air. Somehow, we were able to press beyond the desire to panic, and we went into spiritual warfare mode. On my brother-in-law's behalf, I began to war in the spirit realm. During the three-hour trip, we prayed in the Spirit the entire time. Both my wife and I looked for God to move in a mighty way and show us his glory.

Finally, we got to Charleston. We were almost out of breath as we ran into the hospital to see about JB. We were also almost in tears as we walked into the hospital lobby. There were no words to describe the amazement that we felt as we saw all the family members and friends who showed up to express their loving prayers and support for JB.

JB was a bouncer at a nightclub in Charleston. Apparently, there were some guys that started making trouble and he ended up having to kick them out of the club. These guys were furious about being forced to leave the club. They waited until closing time and came back. While JB was walking two co-workers to their cars, the guys opened fire and began shooting up the place. Several employees and guests got hit. Sixteen of those flying bullets hit JB. He had a bullet lodged in his skull along with several in his forearms and legs. There is no other way to put it, he was in bad shape.

As critical as things seemed for JB, the one thing that I know for sure is that you can never underestimate the power of prayer. Here we were gathered together in the hospital lobby. It was about fifty or so, friends and family members.

The Bible says: "For where two or three are gathered together in My name, there am I in the midst of them." (Matthew 18:20)

Regardless of race, color, gender, or creed, we were all holding hands, touching, and agreeing for the same purpose to ask God to have mercy on JB's life. JB was a very popular kind of guy; he was loved by so many family members and friends. We all wanted to see him pull through this tragic situation.

As the old saying goes, to know JB was to love him. He was a natural-born fighter. He served as a Marine in the military, studied martial arts, and he was just an all-around tough guy. In other words, he was one who loves kicking a_ _ ...if you know what I mean.

With the Lord's help, we knew he would pull through this situation.

Several months later, we were in revival at my church, with the late blind prophet, Bishop L.C. Copeland, founder of the True Destiny Restoration Center. During his message, he stopped and said, "I hear the name Jimmy." There happened to be two

men that we knew named Jimmy: my wife's brother "JB" and a visitor at the church.

Somehow the prophet had picked up on JB in the Spirit and he used the visiting Jimmy as a conduit for prayer and visitation. It was the most amazing thing I had ever seen. We were in North Carolina praying for JB and, all the time in West Virginia, God was working a miracle and answering our prayers through a powerful man of God. Both JB and Jimmy in the congregation were blessed beyond measure.

No doubt it was very hard for our family to see JB near death. On the wings of our prayers, he fought his way back to health. He made it through reconstructive surgery and physical therapy. Currently, he walks with a little limp and uses a walker. Despite, the limp, he is still alive and well. He is full of faith and, every day, he's growing stronger and stronger.

To God be the Glory for his faithfulness.

Points of Faith

- **No matter what happens, God can bring you through it.**

"No weapon that is formed against thee shall prosper; and every tongue that shall rise against thee in judgment thou shalt condemn. This is the heritage of the servants of the Lord, and their righteousness is of Me," saith the Lord." (Isaiah 54:17)

- **Prayer changes everything.**

"Confess your faults one to another, and pray one for another, that ye may be healed. The effectual fervent prayer of a righteous man availeth much." (James 5:16)

- **Don't be afraid to expect a miracle.**

"If ye have faith as a grain of mustard seed, ye shall say unto this mountain, remove hence to yonder place; and it shall remove; and nothing shall be impossible unto you. (Matthew 17:20)

Prayer

Lord, I realize that some things may happen that will literally take my breath away. However, in my breathless state, I will still trust. I know that no weapon formed against me or my family can prosper. I will hide your word in my heart. I will activate my faith by speaking to the mountains in my life and commanding them to remove.

When God Shows Up and Shows Out

"I am realistic. I expect miracles."

Wayne W. Dyer

I have no idea where to begin in sharing this testimony. I don't remember the month, but I do know the exact year.

It was in 2005 that our children asked to go to a school party. Due to the call of God that is on our lives and on our children's destiny, Dyan and I didn't think it was a good idea.

For the first time, I was starting to rethink our decision, because I remembered what it felt like to be considered strange, the weirdo, or not fit in with the crowd because your family was always focused on things of God.

Also, I didn't want our kids to grow up resenting the church. Finally, I was ready to give in and say, "Okay, you can go, but you won't be singing or playing the drums on Sunday morning." I guess in some way, I was hoping that this punishment might make them change their minds.

Looking back, I must admit this was a very difficult challenge for us all. Their mother and I only wanted to set the right example, without compromising our righteousness. However, we also did not want to rob them of their youth. After our family debate, the verdict was still, "No, you can't go."

My wife was dropping the kids off at school. Usually, there's nothing but love in the air, our kids would love on us and tell us goodbye. But this was different. They were mad and upset

that they wouldn't be going to the party. They got out of the car with attitude and slammed the door behind them.

After school, my wife decided to cheer them up by getting some ice cream.

Later on, I received a panic phone call from my wife. She said, "It's bad...get here, quickly." Then she hung up the phone.

Not really knowing which direction to take. I said, "Okay, Lord, I need you to get me there, quickly."

I put my foot on the accelerator and drove with great speed. When I got to the scene, I realized that my wife had been in an accident. She was hit from behind. The force of the impact was so great that it crushed her SUV like a soda can and the rear windshield was knocked completely out. All I could hear were my kids screaming from the pain. They were saying over and over again, "Daddy, help...it hurts." My wife was bruised up pretty bad. But of course, she was more concerned for the kids. The ambulance and fire department arrived, and they assisted in getting my entire family to the hospital.

Once they got to the hospital, they were in separate rooms. My wife was battered and bruised pretty bad, my daughter suffered three broken ribs, and the doctors said my son's back was broken (lumbar 3). It was possible that he would have to learn to walk again.

As you can imagine, I was a little overwhelmed, trembling, yet trusting the Lord to get us through this. I have always been a firm believer that prayer changes everything. I started

calling as many believers as I could who knew how to get a prayer through.

Once my wife got situated in the hospital, she wanted to see the kids. I knew that she really wanted to see our daughter. I explained that our daughter was in pain but she was going to be okay. However, I could not even come up with the words to tell Dyan what was going on with our son. I knew that she would not be able to handle it.

I took her by the hand and led her down the hall. As we walked to our son's room, I shared with her what the doctor said. She was in shock and in disbelief.

When we got to our son's room, he was in good spirits. He was unmoved by the doctor's report. To our surprise, he was calm, cool, and collected. He looked his mother right in the eyes and said, "Mom, I'm fine. I'm going to be just fine."

The doctor on duty had shared the x-rays with us. We could see the fracture where his back was broken and the bones that were separated. Even though we were looking at this shocking evidence, we continued in prayer. We had to believe God for a miracle.

As time went on, there was a shift change. A new doctor came in and she introduced herself to us. She asked, "Do you mind if I take another x-ray?"

Dyan and I were both still trying to get our minds around our son's diagnosis. We told her to take as many x-rays as she needed to take. We needed one of them to line up with the supernatural miracle that we were expecting.

After a while, the doctor returned to our son's room with the new x-ray results. Something was different. It was as if, while God was performing the miracle, the picture was taken and all we could see was a hairline fracture. The fracture was where the bones were coming together. God had performed a miracle right before our eyes. My entire family was able to walk out of the hospital with me.

To God be the Glory!

Points of Faith

- **When things go wrong, we have to believe in those things that we cannot see.**

"As it is written, I have made thee a father of many nations,) before him whom he believed, even God, who quickeneth the dead, and calleth those things which be not as though they were." (Romans 4:17)

- **Pray over every situation and decision.**

"And this is the confidence that we have in him, that, if we ask anything according to his will, he heareth us." (1 John 5:14)

- **You never know which way your miracle is going to come.**

"Jesus replied, "What is impossible with man is possible with God." (Luke 18:27)

Prayer

Lord, I ask you to allow me to hear your voice with clarity. In all chaos and confusion of this world, let me still away from the clutter so that I can hear your divine wisdom and instructions in peace. Let me always stand on the foundation of your word and whatever it is you are saying to me. No matter what it looks like or who disagrees, let me hold sacred what you have spoken in my spirit. Even when my mind doubts, may my faith overshadow the fear and boldly declare, whatever you have spoken shall surely come to pass.

Leap of Faith

*Sometimes your only available
transportation is a leap of faith.*

Margaret Shepard

In 2017, we decided to change the name of our ministry to Greater Faith Ministries of Winston. During this time, the Lord was blowing our minds with tremendous testimonies, miracles, and blessings upon blessings. I am so grateful to God and I'd like to take this time to share one of those amazing miracles and testimonies with you!

Our head deacon had invited his next-door neighbors to service one Sunday. They were a very nice couple from West Africa, Aruna and Dorothy Bockarie. They seemed to really enjoy their worship experience and got connected with the ministry. Not long afterward, they joined the church and became active leaders.

At the time, Aruna and Dorothy had been married for several years and had a strong desire to have children. Approximately, for twelve months or so, they tried to get pregnant, to no avail.

In April 2017, Dorothy started experiencing abdominal pain due to irregular cycles. Her private doctor referred her to a fertility doctor, who ran several tests and discovered that there was a hormonal imbalance and her right fallopian tube was blocked. The doctor gave his professional opinion that she would not be able to have children and that the only solution was surgery.

After hearing the doctor's diagnosis, they decided to stay in faith and stand on the Word of God. Dorothy shared with me that during this season that I was teaching a series about the "Five Foundational Scriptures" for your life, she continued to share their five foundational scriptures with me and how they began to activate their faith by buying baby supplies. Are you hearing me? The doctor says, "There's no way...it's not possible!" But instead of panicking, they chose to pray and believe God. The Bible says, "All things are possible to them that believe."

You know I thank God for the doctors, nurses, and lawyers because they were created for a specific purpose. However, their job is to share with you the facts, based on what they see through technology, the raw data, or evidence of what's in their hands at the moment.

Sometimes, we allow their facts to overtake our faith and cause us to become weary in the fight to believe God for something greater.

The Bible teaches us to maintain our faith at all times, no matter how bad it gets, "For without faith it is impossible to please God." (Hebrews 11:6)

Only God has the power to override the facts through faith! God is able to do the miraculous, the incredible, and the impossible. God uses our faith to fight the facts! He will shift and change the outcome in your favor. But you've got to maintain your faith. Trust and believe that whatever He has promised, He is well able to perform!

Let's get back to Aruna and Dorothy's testimony! Again, the doctors had given their diagnosis that she couldn't have children. Of course, Aruna and Dorothy were a little devastated to hear the news.

However, after sharing the doctor's report with our church family, we all came together as a united front in prayer! We began to bombard Heaven on their behalf and believe God with them for a miracle.

In October 2020, the pain was getting worse, and Dorothy's fertility doctor scheduled the surgery. During her preparation, it is standard procedure to check all female patients for pregnancy before surgery. In disbelief, Dorothy's nurse checked her several times. The test was positive for pregnancy and the surgery was canceled.

On July 1st of 2021, baby Alexander Jedidiah Bockarie was born.

To God be the Glory!

Our God is a God of miracles, in whom there is no respecter of persons. If you are believing God to do something supernatural in your life, here are the foundational scriptures that Aruna and Dorothy applied to their lives.

Points of Faith

- **God has the power to override the facts by faith.**

"Now the Lord was gracious to Sarah as he had said, and the Lord did for Sarah what he had promised. Sarah became pregnant and bore a son to Abraham in his old age, at the very time God had promised him." (Genesis 21:1-2)

- **Maintain your faith - no matter what! Trust and believe that whatever God has promised, He is well able to perform.**

"I prayed for this child, and the Lord has granted me what I asked of him." (1 Samuel 1:27)

- **The power of God's word quickens the barren womb and causes it birth miracles.**

"Lo, children are a heritage of the Lord, and the fruit of the womb is His reward. As arrows are in the hand of a mighty man, so are the children of the youth. Happy is the man that hath his quiver full of them; they shall not be ashamed, but they speak with the enemies at the gate." (Psalm 127: 3-5)

- **Sing O barren - worship while you wait**

"He settles the childless woman in her home as a happy mother of children." (Psalm 113:9)

- **Our God is God of miracles**

"Your children will be like olive shoots around your table." (Psalm 128:3)

Prayer

There are times when things may seem out of my control, but I will stand on your word, that all things are working together for my good and for your glory. That no matter what my problem is, there is an answer in scripture that supports my victory. I will not allow what I see, to change my confession of faith. I know my truth is found in the Word of God. I will not allow my circumstance to cause my faith to falter. But flourish!

An Unexpected Blessing

Don't stop praying. He hears you and He is working it out for your good.

Anonymous

I remember this particular testimony happened early in ministry. I had just taken on the assignment of becoming the interim pastor for Faith Christian Outreach Center in Winston Salem, NC.

The previous pastor was suffering from exhaustion, frustration, and emotional burnout in dealing with the stubbornness of folks in the ministry. It didn't take me long to understand what led to his predicament. As the old saying goes, "You can lead a horse to water but you cannot make it drink." Ministry can be very challenging. It can be exhausting when dealing with the spirits of stiff-necked and stubborn people.

Moses had the same problem in dealing with the children of Israel after he led them out of Egypt. He cried out to God many times on behalf of their stubbornness, murmuring, and complaining. He asked God to be merciful and to pardon their sins. Moses was their intercessor. Yet often times the people talked against him and even considered stoning him.

Other times, he cried out of frustration because his assignment was to lead them to the Promise Land. A journey that should have only taken eleven days wound up taking 40 years because the people he was leading would rather murmur and complain, instead of walking by faith and learning by the example of his leadership. I can imagine that was hard for Moses to endure.

I don't want to get too far off track. Let's get back to the point I want to make in sharing this testimony.

Early in ministry, I had to deal with the people's games of manipulation and control. I was only a few months into taking on this new assignment. I had been thrust into this position when the former pastor had left without giving proper notice.

Can you imagine how the congregation was taking this news? One Sunday, the pastor you love and adore was gone. At that same moment, there was an announcement that the new guy standing before you was taking his place.

There is no way to describe the looks that I received on my first Sunday as minister. The pain of uncertainty was all over their faces. For some, you could see a sigh of relief as they were happy to have somebody, rather than nobody at all. Then there were others that gave me the look of death. The expressions showed their disapproval of my presence. I am sure there were other ministers that were wondering why a stranger was selected and not them.

I had a lot of lessons to learn within a short period of time. The first and most important lesson was handling the finances of the church. When you are an overseer of a ministry, it requires financial support to sustain the church. Most people just attend church. They do not realize that the light bill has to be paid. The water bill and the rent also have to be taken care of on time.

At the time, I was still working a secular day job. My wife also was working. Some of the people in the church felt a sense of empowerment. It was almost as if they were retaliating by withholding their tithes. Their consensus seemed to be "If the pastor doesn't follow our orders or instructions, we'll just refuse to give our tithes and offerings."

My wife and I believe in giving a tithe, which is only ten percent of a person's wages or salary that goes toward the ministry's needs. It ensures that the ministry's financial upkeep is taken care of.

Well, to make a long story short, the day came when the people began to challenge me, my methods, and even the sermons that I was preaching. They would make demands on the type of messages I should preach. But I refused to be persuaded and continued to follow the voice of the Lord and the direction I felt He was giving me to minister to our congregation.

A few members got angry because I would not follow their requests. They retaliated by not giving their tithes and offerings. They didn't leave the church but they just stopped giving and supporting the ministry while continuing to challenge my leadership. It was a tough time for us in ministry but we held on and we kept being strong. My wife and I really couldn't afford it at the time, but we did what we had to do in order to sustain the ministry. Many times, we gave more than the ten percent required. There were also times we made sure the church's bills were paid first, before meeting our own personal needs. We were young in ministry and believed that if we took care of God's house, He would take care of our home. And He did. We did that for a while until things got uncomfortable in our own house.

I worked for one of the fastest-growing banks, Branch Banking & Trust (BB&T), in the city. Every year, during the Christmas holiday, the bank would sponsor a gathering for all the executives, their wives, the employees, and their families to come together to celebrate the birth of Jesus. The word got around, that there was this new guy at the bank who happened to be a pastor and he sang pretty well. I was invited to attend this event to sing during this celebration. The song I chose to

sing was "Mary, Did You Know?" After I sang the song, the crowd was in tears and gave me a standing ovation.

I didn't know that particular song was the favorite of one of the executives.

As I'm shaking hands with all these high-level bank executives, their family members, and friends, one of the top executives approached me. He asked me to follow him to his office. I had no idea what was happening. He began to ask me personal questions about my wife and family. Then he talked about ministry and how involved he was in his church. The more questions he asked, the more I began to realize this was not just a chance incident. This was a God-ordained moment and God was up to something.

Remember, the spirit of manipulation I had to deal with at the church? Well, God was getting ready to wipe all that away.

Within minutes, the executive asked me one question that would change my life. He asked, "How much does it take to run your ministry for an entire year?" Keep in mind, I had not been pastoring for a year, so I wasn't really sure. I thought about what I had spent so far, and I began to pray to the Holy Spirit for a number. Almost as soon as I allowed the number to roll off my tongue, the executive reached into his drawer and pulled out a checkbook. He wrote a check for the exact number that I had given him, and then he handed it to me.

When I think about this, it still makes me tremble. It was almost impossible to hold back the tears. All the ridicule and frustration that I had experienced in stepping into a new role as a pastor at times seemed unbearable. Now, within my fingers, I was holding the answer to most of my prayers. Mostly, I was holding the ability to move my ministry forward with or without the support of some of the members of the congregation who were refusing to be supportive.

To God be the Glory for being a "way maker" out of "no way."

Points of Faith

- **Be specific in your prayers.**

"And Jesus stood still, and called them and said, "What will ye that I shall do unto you?" They said unto Him, "Lord, that our eyes may be opened." So Jesus had compassion on them and touched their eyes, and immediately their eyes received sight, and they followed Him." (Matthew 20: 32-34

- **Trust the Lord no matter what.**

"Have not I commanded thee? Be strong and of a good courage; be not afraid, neither be thou dismayed, for the Lord thy God is with thee whithersoever thou goest." (Joshua 1:9)

- **God will take care of you.**

"And God is able to make all grace abound toward you, that ye, always having all sufficiency in all things, may abound in every good work." (2 Corinthians 9:8)

Prayer

Father, there are many times, life circumstances may seem to be overwhelming, but I will trust you through the process. I will never give up or give out. Please give the grace, when the outcomes of life are not looking so good, to always look upward for strength. Every day my faith is increasing, I am growing stronger in your Word, I realize that you have no limits! My blessings can literally come from anywhere and anybody at any given moment. I am confident that you will take care of me. By faith, I will never doubt your promises of providence or divine provision ever again.

It's Time for a Miracle

Every day holds the possibility of a miracle.

Unknown

When we read the Bible, it is easy to gloss over the miracles that Jesus performed and think that happened only then. However, the reality is that miracles are still happening every day.

The Bible states, "Now unto him that is able to do exceeding abundantly above all that we ask or think, according to the power that worketh in us." (Ephesians 3:20)

This particular scripture certainly sums up my life experiences. I have so many lessons about life and faith; it is hard to keep up with them all. However, there is one that I will never forget.

I was asked to speak at a Sunday evening service for a friend's community event. This particular service was right in the heart of downtown Winston. The primary residents were low- income and many of the folks were struggling with addictions. I cannot recall the actual message of my sermon that night. However, I do recall it was a message about having faith in God beyond your struggles.

During the message, I noticed a man who seemed to have suffered from a stroke. The right side of his face had some paralysis, and his right arm seemed to be shriveled. As I ministered, the presence of God was quite evident in the building. As the word went forth, people were uplifted.

While I was preaching, I could feel this man latching onto every word and his faith being stirred to believe God again.

When I brought my message to a close, it was time for the altar call.

For those of you reading this, who may not be familiar with sermon delivery protocol, the altar call is an open invitation to the congregates after the sermon. This allows anyone who has been touched by the message an opportunity for prayer.

After I finished preaching, I opened the altar up for anybody who was battling depression or those who needed a miracle, healing in the body, or a spiritual breakthrough of any kind. I wanted to see true deliverance take place. I called everyone that needed a breakthrough to come up for prayer.

The Bible says, "For where two or three are gathered together in My name, there am I in the midst of them." (Matthew 18:20)

When the altar call was given, the man who suffered the stroke came up for prayer. We anointed his head with oil and began to believe God with him in prayer. In James 5:16, it states, "Confess your faults one to another, and pray one for another, that ye may be healed. The effectual fervent prayer of a righteous man availeth much."

I kept this scripture in mind, as I prayed. While I was anointing him, I was having a full conversation with the Lord. I remember saying, "God I know you're able…you can do anything…you can heal him…there's nothing impossible for you."

I remember thinking it may take some time. It may take a few months, but I still believed God would do it.

As I began to pray, I could feel a surge of the power of God in the room. This man's faith was in expectation of a miracle. I remember he locked eyes with me. Then all of a sudden, the arm that was shriveled shot straight up in the air. Immediately, God healed this man, by giving him a healing miracle in his

arm and hand. There wasn't a dry eye in the room. Everyone began to weep, rejoice, and celebrate this man's miracle.

I never will forget the rebuke of the Lord that day. It was as if I heard the audible voice of God saying, "Don't you ever put a time stamp on me. I am the God of miracles!"

I had to repent. Even though I thought it was possible, I just didn't think that it would happen right away. I began to repent and asked God to forgive me. I'll never forget the lesson learned that day. Several weeks passed. I was walking downtown and ran into the man that received his miracle.

Without saying a word, he smiled at me and lifted up his arms to celebrate the miracle that God performed in his life.

To God be the Glory!

Points of Faith

- **Never underestimate the power of God.**

"For I am not ashamed of the gospel, because it is the power of God that brings salvation to everyone who believes: first to the Jew, then to the Gentile." (Romans 1: 16)

- **Miracles are still happening today.**

"By stretching forth Thine hand to heal, and that signs and wonders may be done by the name of Thy holy child Jesus." (Acts 4:30)

- **No matter how dark the situation is, always expect God to show up and show out.**

"Now unto him that is able to do exceedingly abundantly above all that we ask or think, according to the power that worketh in us." (Ephesians 3:20)

Prayer

Lord, I truly believe this is the season to walk in miracles. I trust you to take over every aspect of my life. I believe you to do wonderous works in my finances, in my health, in my marriage, in my family and in my ministry. There is no aspect of my life that you cannot change, touch or transform. I cancel all doubt and turn all preconceived notions over to you. From this day forth, I activate my faith to fully believe, that with you all things are possible and that you will not withhold any good thing from me.

Faith for the Family

*Family is not an important thing.
It's everything.*

Michael J. Fox

Throughout this book, I have shared testimonies about faith, but we cannot forget about faith when it comes to our families, especially our children. Many of you who have children may find this chapter to be of particular interest.

I think that since birth, "the measure of faith" has been infused within each of us. Now, there are levels of faith that must be attained, and I am convinced that God intentionally places us in relation to other virtuous people, in the body of Christ at strategic times, for the sole goal and purpose of helping us to discover, cultivate, and exercise our faith.

I said all that, nevertheless, to tell my testimony. My wife and I were very fortunate to be the proud parents of two extraordinarily gifted, talented, and anointed children. Our son, aka Mike Teezy, and our daughter, Dee Marie, both have proven to be tremendous blessings in our lives.

Deanna Marie, our firstborn is Ms. Fearless Fashionista and sings like a mockingbird. She is gifted with beauty and is a very compassionate, vivacious, and lovely young lady. Although she is not particularly large in size, she's feisty and ready to fight to defend what she believes! She is very opinionated, strong-willed, and occasionally stubborn. She is distinctive and has

very unique qualities. You can't disrespect or break her trust, or make her mad. However, she is perfect in every way. She is Daddy's little girl and always will be. My wife and I both love her dearly.

Raising Deanna wasn't easy. At a very young age, she was very determined and tenacious and always felt the need to test the waters, bend the rules, or challenge the instructions. That's just Deanna.

Both our children are grown and on their own now. But occasionally, I like to look back to see where God has brought us from. I am so thankful as parents that we took the time to get to know our kids.

I also appreciate all the family prayer meetings, intimate conversations, get-togethers around the coffee table, and the "dad-prepared" Saturday morning breakfasts. Over the years, I've realized just how important it was to spend time with our kids, to simply be there as a dad. I now realize that it was important to be a shoulder to cry on, to be a hand to hold, to celebrate their successes, to encourage them when they were down, and to know when to say "No." All of these things were crucial to assisting our kids in developing their faith. This was a privilege that I didn't have growing up. However, these things were just as essential to maintaining their faith as weekly sermons from the Word of God.

Let's fast forward the story, our daughter had a pretty tough school year at college and decided to come back home for a while. At this particular period in her life, she was in a position to lead her own life, and attending church was not in her plans.

But we have learned that no matter how old our kids get, parents should never give up on them. We must intercede and provide a prayer covering for them at all times. (I thank God somebody prayed for me.)

I will never forget the Saturday night at two in the morning when our daughter called my wife. She appeared to be in a panic, angry, and distressed state. She was operating a friend's vehicle, and we suspected that she might have been drinking.

I can still hear my wife saying, "Just come home...everything is going to be all right."

"Why does this always happen to me, Mommy?" Deanna asked crying and in a frustrated tone in her voice. "I'm going to be okay, Mom," she said before hanging up.

Minutes later, we received another phone call, telling us that our daughter had been involved in a bad car accident.

Sunday mornings usually find us getting ready to go to church. So, on this specific Sunday, we hurried to church to alert our church family about the incident and ask for intercession.

As we arrived at the hospital, we discovered that she was identified as Jane Doe. You have no idea how horrifying, devastating, and heartbreaking it was to see our baby girl lying there in that condition, connected to breathing monitors, tubes, and IVs all over her body. There was nothing we could do but pray, asking God to intervene and have mercy.

We started to investigate and ask questions regarding the collision. We learned that she had collided head-on with a Mack Truck while traveling at a speed of 70+ mph on the opposite side of the highway. The police who responded to the scene said, "No one could have survived this accident."

Life occasionally brings about unforeseen events that are out of our control. But then, there are times that we're up under spiritual attack because of who we are, or perhaps it would be more accurate to say "whose" we are! Obviously, there is a tremendous call of God on Deanna's life.

Once more, Satan attempted to take our daughter away, but the prayers of the righteous availeth much and release supernatural power. We're all works in progress, and I am glad to announce that Deanna is alive and well, bruised but not broken, and back in the church.

God has promised us that He will perfect the things that concern our daughter's life. He is faithful to finish the work He has started. God doesn't start anything that He cannot finish. No weapon formed against our little girl will prosper. We are so proud of you, baby girl. Continue to hold onto God's unchanging hand.

Points of Faith

- **We have to trust God to protect our family.**

"No weapon that is formed against thee shall prosper; and every tongue that shall rise against thee in judgment thou shalt condemn. This is the heritage of the servants of the Lord, and their righteousness is of Me," saith the Lord." (Isaiah 54:17)

- **Even when we are not with our children and we cannot guide their decisions, we have to believe that God will.**

"But thus saith the Lord: "Even the captives of the mighty shall be taken away, and the prey of the terrible shall be delivered; for I will contend with him that contendeth with thee, and I will save thy children." (Isaiah 49:25)

- **It is our duty as parents or spiritual guardians to raise our children and help raise the next generation of Kingdom leaders.**

"Train up a child in the way he should go, and when he is old he will not depart from it." (Proverbs 22:6)

Prayer

Lord, we have to have faith in you in every aspect of our lives, including our families. As we stretch our faith to grow in you, let it begin with those that are closest to us. As our children mature and even leave our care, we know that they are not out of your sight. It is our ultimate desire as parents to protect and shield our children from harm. Yet, Lord, we realize every day as we send them out into the world, no matter how young or old we relinquish them to your care, we know they will be safely guided, guarded and protected by your sovereign hand, no matter what.

About the Author

Rev. Michael Lloyd Tyree was born on June 26th, 1965, in the small town of Beckley, West Virginia.

He currently serves as the Senior Pastor and Founder of Greater Faith Ministries of Winston-Salem, North Carolina. He and his lovely wife of 36 years, Lady Dyan, are a dynamic duo working together in ministry.

Pastor Tyree is a very gifted, talented, and anointed man of God. He is a worship leader, talented singer/songwriter, excellent graphic designer, and founder and CEO of MTGRAPHIX Creative Group.

He is a man of great vision and has assisted many leaders, business owners, authors, and entrepreneurs in birthing their dreams and visions. He considers it an honor to partner with people and to see the handiwork of God work through him.

He is the proud father of two children, a daughter Deanna aka singer "DEEMARIE" and a son Michael aka gospel artist "MIKE TEEZY." He is also the proud "G-Poppa" to a granddaughter, little Ms. Nevaeh.

Author's Contact Information

Pastor Michael Tyree

3780 Bethania Station Road Winston-Salem NC 27106

Website:

www.pastortyreeministries.net

Email:

pastortyreeofficial@gmail.com

Church Website:

www.greaterfaithws.com

Made in the USA
Columbia, SC
27 September 2024